SUCH
LOVE
HAVE
NO FEAR

Dispelling Fear and Walking In Boldness

REV. DENISE A. DALRYMPLE, ESQ.

Printed in the United States of America

First Printing, 2021

Follow Pastor Denise Dalrymple on social media

Instagram: pastordenise_d

Facebook: Denise Dalrymple

ISBN: 978-0-578-86172-2

Forward

Are you not reaching your full potential in life? Have you been afraid to move forward, thinking you are not able to achieve? Learn how to overcome the spirit of fear and walk in the power and anointing of God. Walk in the boldness and authority of God so you can reap and enjoy the life that God has promised to you.

2 Timothy 1:7 says:
For God has not given us the
spirit of fear but of love,
power and a sound mind.

My daughter, Pastor Denise Dalrymple, Esq., has truly amazed me. I have watched her develop and grow from a shy and timid young lady into a powerful woman of God. Such Love Have No Fear has been written under the anointing of the Holy Spirit and thus, will radically change your life. Get ready to be encouraged, inspired, and delivered from a world of fear and timidity into a world of power, boldness, and authority.

Bishop Lawrence A. Dalrymple, Sr.
Bethel Worship Center
North Lauderdale, Florida

Dedication

I dedicate this book to my parents, Bishop Lawrence A. Dalrymple, Sr. and the late Dr. Ina L. Dalrymple. They have always instilled in me the Word of God, prayer, and living a faithful life to the Lord. They have given me so much love and support that I am truly grateful.

I also want to dedicate this book to my late brother Lawrence A. Dalrymple, Jr. and also my nephew Lawrence A. Dalrymple, III, who have both been a constant source of strength and encouragement to me.

Acknowledgements

I wish to express my gratitude first and foremost to God, who enabled and guided me to write this book.

I am so grateful to my Dad, Bishop Lawrence A. Dalrymple, Sr., who has supported me and encouraged me to complete this task.

Very special thanks to the following inspirational individuals:

Bishop George G. Bloomer, Presiding Prelate of C.L.U.R.T International Assemblies, Inc., and Pastor of Bethel Family Worship Center, Durham, North Carolina, for inspiring me to learn and study the Word of God.

Dr. Kevin A. Williams, Bishop of New Jerusalem Cathedral and NewJC Nation, Greensboro, North Carolina, for propelling so many, including me, into achieving and stepping out of one's comfort zone.

Also, the genuine support and encouragement of my church family at Bethel Worship Center has been invaluable.

Finally, to a group of individuals who I call my A-Team – Thank you!

Table of Contents

Introduction

Where God's love is, there is no fear, because God's perfect love takes away fear. It is His punishment that makes a person fear. So His love is not made perfect in the one who has fear.

1 John 4:18 ERV

As I recall the day that I accepted Jesus as my Savior, hearing about how much God loved me that He sent His only begotten Son, Jesus, to die just for me. I was in awe that God loved me that much. Keep in mind that I was only 9 years old, and this greatly impacted me. All I could think was that this great big God knew me a long time ago before I knew Him, and He loved me! Wow, at 9 years old, that was tremendous. However, at that age, I never really understood what God's love truly meant.

Growing up as a child, I was timid. I did not speak to anyone unless spoken to. And when spoken to, I would be polite and respond by saying their name and a one-word response. If someone said, Hello Denise, my response is

Hello and their name. If someone said, How are you? My response was fine, and their name. That was it.

There was a class play in elementary school that my teacher chose me to recite a one-line speaking part. I told her, very politely, no. She said yes, this would be good for me. Of course, I could not see how this would be good for me. But my parents were elated that I had a part in the play. As I grew older, I believed her intentions were good, but I knew at that time that I could not do it. The practices we had leading up to the night of the play were horrible but she still believed that I could say this one line in front of many people. The night of the play has arrived, and it is time for me to say my one line. Instead of me saying the one line, I looked at the crowd, fear came over me, and I ran off the stage. There was a staircase nearby leading to the audience, and so I ran towards the staircase. My dad saw me, and when I saw him at the bottom of the staircase, I flew into his arms. Thank God, he caught me. There was a side door leading outside, and so my dad took me outside for air. Good move on his part, because for a moment I became ill and threw up. The shyness and fear overcame me. I was only 7 at the time. After this experience, I was so afraid to speak in public, and I continued in life, walking in fear, only accomplishing things that I felt comfortable doing. Definitely not having to do anything publicly.

As I grew older, our Church in New York would have plays and skits that we would participate in as teenagers. Of course, except me. My youth leaders would always ask me, and I would say no. However, our Church did a puppet show one time, and those who participated were not seen, only heard. To everyone's surprise, including me, I volunteered to participate to be one of the voices. Everyone could not believe that I did such an awesome job. They said I spoke clearly and loudly with such feelings and emotions. Even I enjoyed performing. What I loved was that I could speak, and no one could see me. You see my mindset.

Growing up, my parents taught me the importance of working hard and getting a good education. So I did just that. I graduated from High School at 16, continued my education at Adelphi University, and began working full time at a local bank as a bank teller. As I continued to work full-time, at the age of 19, I graduated with my Bachelor's in Money Management with a concentration in Corporate Finance and Investments. A year later, I obtained my Master of Business Administration and then continued to complete law school, passed the bar, and became an attorney. But in accomplishing all of this, I would barely speak or participate in any of my classes, always sitting in the back of the classroom. A silent student was I.

See, some of you think that if I decided to become an attorney, I love to talk publicly. How else could you be an attorney? Well, that is a good thought for others, but not for me. In my mind, I could be an attorney but do only transactional work, and therefore, I do not have to go to court and speak in front of the Judge. Again, you see my mindset.

I remember in college, public speaking was a required class that I dreaded since we had to recite our speeches in front of the class. That was definitely not for me! It was not something that I wanted to do at all, but I had to, so I did.

One day at the end of the semester, my public speaking professor called me into his office and asked me, what are my career plans? I told him that I plan to attend law school and become a corporate lawyer handling transactional work. He told me that was great but that I needed to do public speaking for a living. Oh man, did I laugh and thought to myself, he is out of his mind. I politely told him, No, that is definitely not me. I am way too shy for that, plus I have nothing to say. He said you don't understand. You have a gift that you hold people's attention when you are speaking. I totally disagreed with him, thanked him for such kind words, and left his office. Well, God definitely has a sense of humor because today, I am pastoring a church in South Florida, and I am a speaker and author.

In the past, I had always limited myself. I always thought this was just because I was timid and quiet as a child. But as I grew older, I realized this was not just shyness but also fear. Fear of failing, fear of the unknown, fear of not being good enough, fear that someone is better than me, fear that I cannot achieve, fear that I do not know enough, fear that I would say the wrong thing or not speak properly – FEAR! What is Fear? Fear is False Evidence Appearing Real.

When fear grips you like this, you limit yourself in what

you can accomplish. Fear grips and stifles you to the point that you miss opportunities that would make you progress further in life. I view it as a slow death from an abundant life. Every time we allow fear to take control of us, we have just set back our life from moving forward to where God wants us to be. We forfeit on living the life that God has truly planned for us. All because of Fear! Fear of the unknown – I have to be in control. Fear of feeling inadequate – I can't do it; I am not capable of doing that. Fear of thinking that I should play it safe – do what I know I can handle and accomplish. Fear of, oh no, not me! Fear of, but I am not as good as so and so. Fear!

Jesus said in John 10:10,

A thief comes to steal, kill, and destroy.
*But I came to give life-life that is full and good.- **ERV***

When we walk in fear, we have allowed Satan to steal, kill and destroy what we need to accomplish. Satan wants us to be intimidated, and when we open the door of our life to him, he comes in to ruin us. In essence, we have allowed Satan to tear down that life of abundance and fullness that God has for us. When we walk in fear, we will never accomplish or live that life of victory that God has planned for us from before the foundation of the world. In Psalms 139, David realized just how powerful and mighty God is and that through God, his life was all prepared before he (David) lived one day. That is the kind of love that our God has for us.

The word of God tells us, "Where God's love is, there is <u>NO</u> fear, because God's perfect love takes away fear." 1 John 4:18(a) ERV *Emphasis Added*. As a believer, I realized that I should not be walking in fear because I have the love of God in my life. And because I have the love of God in my life, I can do all things. I have the ultimate supreme power working in me and through me. Wow! That is the kind of love that **My God** has for me!!!

I should be living the life that God has planned for me, and God will make sure that it is accomplished in my life if I love and trust in Him. I have no reason to fear. But this also meant that I needed to understand God's love for me and how to perfect it in me. 1 John 4:18 continues to say, "So His *(God's love)* is not made perfect in the one who has fear." *Emphasis Added.* So because this is true, we need to dispel all fear and walk in boldness!

Today, understanding this, I am walking in God's perfect love and not in fear. I am walking in the path that God has for me. To me, this means moving into the unknown, relying on the Holy Spirit moment by moment, day by day for directions, following what He wants to accomplish through me, and ultimately living the victorious life God has for me.

My Prayer For You:

Heavenly Father, I pray for everyone who is reading this book. I pray that You, Lord, will remove the spirit of fear, doubt, and uncertainty from their lives, but fill their lives with the spirit of boldness, courage and power. Lord, as You have changed my life, I pray that You, Lord, will radically change their lives from living a fearful life to living a life of boldness, success, and victory.

In Jesus Name, Amen!

Chapter 1

God's Message Of Love

God's Message Of Love

For God so loved the world that He gave His only begotten Son, that whoever believes in Him should not perish but have everlasting life. For God did not send His Son into the world to condemn the world, but that the world through Him might be saved.

John 3:16-17 NKJV

Looking into the ocean, you see a vast volume of water that continues into infinity. How far does it go? How deep is it? Does one truly know? One's eyes cannot see from the shores of the ocean how far the ocean is. Yet even if you venture to the horizon and think that you are reaching the line, you look again, and the horizon is once again farther than you can imagine. The sun penetrates the ocean with just enough rays to warm it. The moon extracts just enough gravity to keep the ocean in its place.

The ocean waves come rolling in as if the water knows exactly where to go and when to stop. The seagulls fly over the ocean and scoop low enough not to touch the water until the opportune time is to either catch a fish or enjoy bathing in the ocean. The white sand fills the shores so that man can walk and lie on the sand without sinking to the earth's core. God created all of this and so much more. Why? It is simple. God loves us.

God decided to create day and night, the waters, the heaven, the earth, the sun and the moon, the creatures in the waters, the birds in the air, and the living creatures on the land. After seeing how beautiful and good everything was, God called Jesus and the Holy Spirit together and said it is time to create man in our image. Why? It is simple. God loves us.

God provided a perfect beautiful Garden for us to live and enjoy without any problems, issues, or challenges to face. He made all sorts of trees that were good for food and pleasing to the eye. God also created rivers that would water the trees in the Garden so we would eternally enjoy them. To top it off, God even placed in the center of the Garden the Tree Of Life. Then God placed man and woman in the Garden and said, for your own good, do not eat "of The Tree Of The Knowledge Of Good And Evil" because if you do, you will surely die. Why? It is simple. God loves us.

With all the trees in the beautiful perfect Garden, man decided not to listen to God and instead ate from the only tree that God said not to. We had the opportunity not to be disobedient and sinful but decided to be disobedient. After eating "of The Tree of The Knowledge Of Good And Evil," we became like God, Jesus, and the Holy Spirit where we must know how to distinguish between good and evil and blessings and calamity. Thus, because of sin and disobedience, man was taken from the Garden. Although God loves us, He cannot look upon sin. This pained God but God still did not turn His back on us. Why? It is simple. God loves us.

As man was living on the earth, man was growing further and further from God, and there was a bridge between God and man because of sin. But even though we were disobedient and destroyed our relationship with God, He wanted to have a relationship with us. Consequently, God sacrificed someone so dear to Him so that we can once again have communion with Him. Why? It is simple. God loves us.

In John 3:16, Jesus says,

"For God so loved the world that He gave His only begotten Son and whoever believes in Him should not perish but have eternal life."

NKJV

Even though we disobeyed God and turned from Him, God had great compassion for us that He allowed us the opportunity to be reconciled with Him through His Son, Jesus Christ. He gave us the opportunity to have eternal life and defeat death. He gave us the opportunity to talk with Him, walk with Him and fellowship with Him, again. He gave us the opportunity to live rich, wealthy, victorious, and abundant lives on earth, just like in the Garden.

That is why Jesus said, in John 10:10(b),

"For I have come to give **YOU** *life and life more abundantly."*

ESV

Jesus was not just talking about eternal life but victorious living now today in our daily lives. Why? It is simple. God loves us!

Abundant living is mine!!! Abundant living is yours!!! This means that, as a believer, I am more than a conqueror. This means I have no reason to fear. This means that God is with me wherever I go. This means I can fulfill the assignments and plans that God has prepared for me.

This sounds so simple and something we all know, but why do we walk and live our lives in fear? Why do we walk around with a defeated spirit, attitude, and mindset? Why do we feel that we are inadequate to accomplish the tremendous things in our lives? Why do we allow God in some areas of our lives but not in every area? Why do we feel that God can handle simple issues in our life but not the complicated and difficult ones? Why do we try to fix the issue or the challenges that come our way instead of letting the issue and challenge solver do it? Why do we confine God in a box and limit what He wants to do for us and through us? When all along God is saying, I am here for you. Do not be afraid! Do not fear! But walk in my boldness, courage, and power! Ask whatever you want in My will and in faith believing, and it shall be granted unto you.

God is saying, I have made you the head and not the tail, above and not beneath, the lender and not the borrower. I have made you that you shall flourish and prosper because you are a tree living by the streams of My waters. I have made you priests and kings, a royal priesthood, and a Holy Nation.

I AM Jehovah Raah, Your Shepherd, so you lack nothing. I AM Jehovah Rapha, Your Healer, of all your sicknesses and diseases, so walk in health and strength. I AM Jehovah Jireh, Your Provider, so all your needs shall be provided. I AM Jehovah Shalom, Your Peace, so you have *MY* peace. I AM Jehovah Nissi, Your Banner, so I fight your battles for you. I AM Jehovah Shammah, the God who is always there for you. I AM the Maker of heaven and earth, so your foot will not slip or be moved. I AM Your God, so no weapon formed against you shall prosper, and any tongue that rises up in judgment against you shall be condemned. I AM Your Vindicator; therefore, you do not live in condemnation. I AM Your Acquitter, so you have the peace of reconciliation to hold and enjoy. I AM Your Strength, so you never have to be weak. Why? It is simple.

God loves us.

The beautiful aspect of God's love for us is that the Word of God tells us that nothing shall separate us from the love of God. The Apostle Paul says it so beautifully:

God knew what He was doing from the very beginning. He decided from the outset to shape the lives of those who love Him along the same lines as the life of His Son. The Son stands first in the line of humanity He restored. We see the original and intended shape of our lives there in Him. After God made that decision of what His children should be like, He followed it up by calling people by name. After He called them by name, He set them on a solid basis with Himself. And then, after getting them established, He stayed with them to the end, gloriously completing what He had begun. So, what do you think? With God on our side like this, how can we lose? If God didn't hesitate to put everything on the line for us, embracing our condition and exposing Himself to the worst by sending His own Son, is there anything else He wouldn't gladly and freely do for us? And who would dare tangle with God by messing with one of God's chosen? Who would dare even to point a finger? The One who died for us—who was raised to life for us!—is in the presence of God at this very moment sticking up for us. Do you think anyone is going to be able to drive a wedge between us and Christ's love for us? There is no way! Not trouble, not hard times, not hatred, not hunger, not homelessness, not bullying threats, not backstabbing, not even the worst sins listed in Scripture: They kill us in cold blood because they hate you. We're sitting ducks; they pick us off one by one. None of this fazes us because Jesus loves us. I'm absolutely convinced that nothing—nothing living or dead, angelic or demonic, today or tomorrow, high or low, thinkable or unthinkable—absolutely nothing can get between us and God's love because of the way that Jesus our Master has embraced us.

Romans 8:29-39 MSG

The Apostle Paul knew and understood God's great love in his life and what that meant for him in his life. We all have to grow into understanding God's love for us. Establishing, leaning, basking, and perfecting His love in us.

Growing up, I never had to ask myself the question, did my parents love me. I just knew it because they told me and they showed me. My parents would give me numerous hugs and kisses and tell me how much they loved me. There was a game my mom used to play with me as a child. She would ask me how much does mommy love you? I would hold out my arms as wide as possible and say, this is how much mommy loves me. Why did she do this? It is simple. She loved me.

In December 2002, my mom went home to be with the Lord, but I always sense and feel her love for me to this day. It is a feeling that will never leave me. I can confidently say that I know what it is to experience a mother's true love.

My parents provided for me all the things that a child would need and desire. They would teach me how to be a beautiful woman in society. They would guide me and show me what is best for me. They would give me their very best at whatever sacrifice to them. They would stop what they are doing to be there for me. They would advise me and guide me so I would not make the same mistakes as they did. They would give their last dollar for me. They would give me the world if they could. Why? It is simple. They loved me.

If my parents, who are limited in their resources and provisions and are limited in their thinking and actions, were willing to do so much for me, think about God, who loves me and is limitless in resources and provisions, what He is willing to do for me.

Do any of you have a son? If he asked for bread, would you give him a rock? Or if he asked for a fish, would you give him a snake? Of course not! You people are so bad, but you still know how to give good things to your children. So surely your heavenly Father will give good things to those who ask Him.

Matthew 7:9-11 ERV

Am I saying that God is a Santa Claus? Absolutely not!!! Am I saying that God is a genie? No way!!! I am saying that God loves us more than we can truly comprehend and that God has no limits and no boundaries and because we are His creation and His children, His love for us is limitless. So stop walking in fear. Stop limiting God. Stop putting Him in a box and allow God to do everything His Word says He will do for you. What God has set out for you from before the foundation of the world shall come forth! Prove God, Prove His Word and Prove His Love. Tell yourself that greater works will you do. Stop for just one moment and decide to seek God for your life. God is intentional about completing His plan in the lives of His children. How quickly you get there remains to be determined by you. Ask yourself the questions: "Who do you serve?" "Who do you love?"

A Prayer:

Heavenly Father, thank You for loving me with such great love. Thank You for allowing Your Son, Jesus Christ, to die just for me. Because of Your love for me, I know that I do not have to walk in fear but instead walk in boldness and power.

In Jesus Name, Amen!

Chapter 2

Such Love

Such Love

So, what do you think? With God on our side like this, how can we lose? If God didn't hesitate to put everything on the line for us, embracing our condition and exposing Himself to the worst by sending His own Son, is there anything else He wouldn't gladly and freely do for us? And who would dare tangle with God by messing with one of God's chosen? Who would dare even to point a finger? The One who died for us—Who was raised to life for us!—is in the presence of God at this very moment sticking up for us. Do you think anyone is going to be able to drive a wedge between us and Christ's love for us? There is no way!

Romans 8:31-37 MSG

Nothing can compare to the love that God has for us. Although sin should have kept us separated from God, He loved us so much that He wanted us to be reconciled to Him. This is a distinct, unique, and powerful love.

In Greek, different types of love are mentioned in the Scriptures, and all of them come from God. There is *Eros* that is romantic or sexual love. *Phileo* is a friendship type of love, and *Storge* is love among family members or loyalty. All of these types of love are wonderful and are demonstrated in our lives. But none of these types of love is the love that

God demonstrated to us.

> *But God demonstrates His own love toward us, in that while we were still sinners, Christ died for us.*
>
> ### Romans 5:8 NKJV

God's love is known as *Agape Love*. This *Agape Love* was demonstrated to us by God sending *His Only Begotten Son, Jesus Christ*, to die for you and me, even though we were sinners. And to culminate this, God raised His Son from the dead, and thus, Jesus was resurrected triumphantly.

Agape Love is God's love for us that is an unconditional sacrificial love. This is a perfect, complete, and full-grown love that God has for His children.

> *See what an incredible quality of love*
> *the Father (God) has shown to us,*
> *that we would [be permitted to]*
> *be named and called and counted the*
> *children of God! And so we are!*
>
> ### 1 John 3:1(a) AMP Emphasis Added

It is God's Son going to the cross for us, taking the complete sin of all of mankind. It is God's Son suffering and dying on the cross for us so we can have the forgiveness and pardon of our sins and thus being in right standing with God. It is God's Son being resurrected with all power of the Holy Spirit, and now God's Son is sitting at God's right hand interceding on God's children's, our, behalf. All this was done even though we do not deserve it. There is nothing we did to get it, and we cannot demand it. Neither can we buy it or earn it. But God extends it to us anyway.

*I mean that you have been saved by grace
because you believed. You did not save
yourselves; it was a gift from God.
You are not saved by the things you have
done, so there is nothing to boast about*

Ephesians 2:8-9 ERV

It is not based on emotion, affection, or even approval. It is unconditional and sacrificial. It is free to anyone willing to accept it.

*Yes, God loved the world so much that He gave His only Son, so
that everyone who believes in Him would not be lost but have eternal
life. God sent His Son into the world. He did not send Him to judge
the world guilty, but to save the world through Him.*

John 3:16-17 ERV

Agape Love makes eternal salvation possible. When we accept Jesus as our Lord and Savior, we receive the *Agape Love* of God into our lives, and we have the capacity to love in the same way God loves.

The Apostle Paul tells the Romans that this *Agape Love* God has for His children is so strong and powerful that there is nothing greater. We are protected. We are covered against all outside influence because nothing can separate us from *God's Agape Love*. And because nothing can separate us from *His Love,* we are more than conquerors. We have complete victory through *God's Agape Love*.

But in all these troubles we have complete victory through God, who has shown His love for us.

Romans 8:37 ERV

According to the Merriam-Webster Dictionary, a conqueror is defined as one who conquers; one who wins a country in war, subdues or subjugates a people, or overcomes an adversary. The KJV Dictionary defines conqueror as one who conquerors; one who gains victory; one who subdues and brings into subjection or possession, by force or by influence. Notice that these definitions tell us what a conqueror means, but the Word of God tells us that in God's *Agape Love*, we are <u>more</u> than a conqueror. In God's *Agape Love*, we <u>more</u> than overcome our adversary, Satan, who wants us to walk our lives in fear and powerlessness. In God's *Agape Love*, we <u>more</u> than overcome and win against all odds. In God's *Agape Love*, we more than overcome any weakness in failing to achieve. In God's *Agape Love*, we are winners; we are victors; we are masters in our own right. We master our adversary's challenges, which includes that attack of the spirit of fear. Therefore, we can walk in boldness and confidence that we can and will accomplish anything and everything.

Nay, in all these things we are
MORE THAN CONQUERORS
through Him that loved us
Romans 8:37 Emphasis Added

Fear is not of God and is not embedded in *God's Agape Love*. Just the opposite. In *God's Agape Love,* we have boldness, confidence, surety, assurance, certainty, fearlessness, valiant, audacity, courage, bravery, positive self-esteem, and so much more! With all of this, then nothing is impossible. This is the *Agape Love* that God has for us.

In 1 Corinthians 13, what is known as The Love Chapter, the Apostle Paul expresses how *God's Agape Love* is greater than anything else under the sun. There is nothing greater in creation than *God's Agape Love*, both receiving and giving of it. *This Love* is greater than being able to speak in tongues, prophesy, and sacrifice everything a person owned or even being able to give one's life. The Apostle Paul wanted his Corinthian brothers and sisters to understand that a major part of following Jesus is love. But to love differently than *Eros*, *Phileo*, or *Storge*. Those love have their place, but *Agape Love* surpasses them all.

In this scripture, and something we will discuss in a future chapter, the Apostle Paul wanted us to know that following Jesus is more than merely being connected to God through Jesus, His Son. He wanted us to know that this *Agape Love* is a transformational love. *God's Agape Love* transforms us to be the people God created us to be on this earth.

God has made us what we are. In Christ Jesus, God made us new people so that we would spend our lives doing the good things He had already planned for us to do.

Ephesians 2:10 ERV

Through transformation, we are perfecting *God's Agape Love* in us. Perfect love cast out all fear.

God is love. When we take up permanent residence in a life of love, we live in God and God lives in us. This way, love has the run of the house, becomes at home and mature in us, so that we're free of worry on Judgment Day-our standing in the world is identical with Christ's. There is no room in love for fear. Well-formed love banishes fear. Since fear is crippling, a fearful life- fear of death, fear of judgment- is one not yet fully formed in love.

1 John 4:17-19 MSG

This is perfect love, complete, full-grown love, *God's Agape Love*. Think of this as an example of perfecting love. When a couple first gets married, they love each other, but there is a fear. Will this work? Will this last? After a while, as they understand and know each other better, then that fear goes, and the relationship becomes one of boldness confidence that the other is not going anywhere. That is the confidence and boldness we need to walk in as we live our lives in *God's Agape Love*.

God's Agape Love requires a response. What is your response? Let's look at Jesus' response to His Father's Love.

Prayer:

Heavenly Father, thank You for such a powerful, perfect, complete, full-grown love that you have demonstrated towards me. I pray that I will learn to walk in this love and live a life of a "More Than A Conqueror."

In Jesus Name, Amen!

Chapter 3

Jesus' Response To His Father's Love

Jesus' Response To His Father's Love

In the beginning, before the earth was made, the Word was there. The Word was with God, and the Word was God. He was there with God in the beginning.

John 1:1-2 ERV

As a believer, whom we desire to exemplify and follow after is Jesus. We should desire to be more like Him. So what is His response to His Father's love to Him? What was the relationship between Jesus and His Father?

In your life together, think the way Christ Jesus thought. He was like God in every way, but He did not think that His being equal with God was something to use for His own benefit. Instead, He gave up everything, even His place with God. He accepted the role of a servant, appearing in human form. During His life as a man, He humbled Himself by being fully obedient to God, even when that caused His death-death on a cross. So God raised Him up to the most important place and gave Him the name that is greater than any other name.

Philippians 2:5-9 ERV

Jesus, God incarnate, came to the earth to fulfill an assignment God, His Father, gave to Him. Jesus, a willing vessel, believed in and was secured in His Father's love and, thus, had faith in His Father's love for Him.

For the Father (God) dearly loves the Son (Jesus) and shows Him everything that He Himself is doing.

John 5:20(a) AMP Emphasis Added

Jesus knew the assignment that His Father gave Him was difficult and would ultimately result in Him giving up His life, but Jesus also knew the love that His Father had for Him. Consequently, Jesus spoke highly of His Father and reciprocated the love of His Father.

But so that the world may know [without any doubt] that I love the Father, I do exactly as the Father has commanded Me [and act in full agreement with Him]. Get up, let us go from here.

John 14:31 AMP

Throughout the scripture, we see that Jesus always followed His Father's direction. He was obedient to His Father's assignment at all costs. Jesus said,

I came down from heaven to do what God wants, not what I want.

John 6:38 ERV

Jesus knew that no matter what, that He was secured in His Father's love. This included the fact that His Father was always there for Him and would never leave Him nor forsake Him. Even when the situation was too much for Jesus to bear, He said to His Father:

> *"Father, if you are willing, please don't make*
> *me drink from this cup. But do what*
> *You want, not what I want."*
>
> ### Luke 22:42 ERV

Jesus was so dependent upon His Father.

> *But Jesus answered, "I assure you that the Son*
> *can do nothing alone. He does only what*
> *He sees His Father doing. The Son does*
> *the same things that the Father does."*
>
> ### John 5:19 ERV

How did Jesus respond to His Father's love? He responded in love, obedience, confidence, faithfulness, and security in His Father. Let's look at the story of when the wind and the wave obeyed Jesus.

Wind And Wave Obey Jesus

> *On the same day, when evening had come, He said to them (the*
> *Twelve - Disciples), "Let us cross over to the other side." Now when*

they had left the multitude, they took Him along in the boat as He was. And other little boats were also with Him. And a great windstorm arose, and the waves beat into the boat, so that it was now full. But He was in the stern, asleep on a pillow. And they awoke Him and said to Him, "Teacher, do You not care that we are perishing?" Then He arose and rebuked the wind, and said to the sea, "Peace, be still!" And the wind ceased and there was a great calm. But He said to them, "Why are you so fearful? How is it that you have no faith?" And they feared exceedingly and said to one another, "Who can this be, that even the wind and the sea obey Him!"

Mark 4:35-41 NKJV Emphasis Added

In the scriptures before Mark 4, Jesus was healing the sick and casting out demons. Jesus gave testimonies to the crowds that He was the Son of God, and He taught the people about God's Kingdom.

On this day, Jesus is teaching the people through parables on the lakeside of the Sea of Galilee. It is evening time, and the sun is beginning to set. Jesus said to the disciples, "Let us cross over to the other side." Jesus said to them that they need to go over to the other side of the Sea of Galilee. What Jesus said to the disciples was very simple, clear and, absolutely unambiguous.

As they were heading over to the other side in the boat, a great storm arose. You have to remember, this is The Sea of Galilee, and this Sea is known for its unexpected sudden and severe storms. Water turbulence would often occur due to the winds that would funnel through the passes and canyons from the surrounding hills. As experienced fishermen, the Disciples knew this. As a matter of fact, all fishermen knew of this risk in their profession. In essence, storms were common. The question was the severity of the storm.

In this story, the storm was severe, and the Disciples became fearful. Water was coming into the boat, and filing up the boat and they believed they would sink. The Disciples believed that they were at the point of death. So they called their Teacher.

Jesus wakes up and, the Disciples say to Him, Do you not care that we perish? Jesus rebuked the wind and said to the sea, "PEACE BE STILL." In Greek this means SILENT! HUSH! The wind and the sea instantly become calm. They were silenced; they were hushed.

Jesus asked his disciples, "Why are you so fearful? You have no faith?" Then the Disciples say, to one another, "Who can this be that even the wind and the sea obey Him?" They wanted to know, What Manner of Man Is This? Even though Jesus and His Disciples were experiencing the same situation, they reacted differently. Why?

Jesus was resting in the midst of the storm because *HE KNEW* without a doubt that He would certainly get to the other side even though chaos and near-death were happening. Jesus had faith in His Father, resulting in Jesus resting in knowing. He is God, and it is going to be all right. But His disciples were worrying and became fearful in the same situation because they did not know. Where was their faith? Jesus said, let's go to the other side. Jesus would not allow them to go into the boat to drown and die. NO. The Disciples allowed fear to take hold of them instead of relying on Jesus who was right there in the boat with them.

But Jesus! He rested in knowing that His Father would take Him through. Why because His Father loved Him and will always be there for Him to make sure that His assignment was complete. Jesus had faith in His Father and had no reason to fear about a storm.

Listen, because of the love of God in our lives and our response to His love; we have no reason to fear. Stop looking at what you believe you can do or accomplish and start rest in knowing that you will achieve with God.

Rest In Knowing. God has you covered. Everything is going to be all right. He has not left you nor forsaken you. What He said He would do, He will do. God is there to make sure that the assignment and plans He has for you get completed. Where is your faith?

Remember, Jesus is our ultimate example, and we know that Jesus exemplified how one should live depending on God and His faithfulness.

Parable Of The Mustard Seed

And the apostles said to the Lord, "Increase our faith!" So the Lord said, "If you have faith as a mustard seed, you can say to this mulberry tree, 'Be pulled up by the roots and be planted in the sea,' and it would obey you.

Luke 17:5-6 NKJV

When the Apostles said to Jesus, increase our faith. Jesus said to them, "If you had faith as a grain of mustard seed..." What does faith as a grain of mustard seed mean? Often when we talk about faith as a grain of mustard seed, we talk about the size of a mustard seed. Mustard seeds are the tiniest seed, usually about 1 to 2 millimeters in diameter. However, the mustard plant is a fast-growing annual herb, growing up to 10 to 12 feet tall in only a few months. Although it is the tiniest seed, it is a powerful seed. So the size of a mustard seed is only one of its characteristics.

Another characteristic of a mustard seed is that it does not cross-pollinate. It is a potent seed. Generally, in gardens, many vegetables will take on the characteristics of other plants surrounding them if the seeds are growing close to each other. This is called cross-pollination.

However, the mustard seed is not like that. A mustard seed can be planted on top of another seed, and it will still be the same, mustard. It will not take on any other seed's characteristics, no matter how close they may grow together. That is a strong powerful seed! In essence, the quality, not the quantity of the faith, is what matters.

In other words, faith as a grain of a mustard seed means growing to a level where we have NO DOUBT in what we believe and who we trust. James 1:6 says,

"But let him ask in Faith, nothing wavering. For he who wavers is like a wave of the sea driven with the wind and tossed."

KJV

We should have faith that is unwavering, unmovable, unshakeable, confident, assurance in our God! No matter what the conditions around us, our faith should stay focused on Jesus and His will, trusting that He is in control, and we should be unaffected by our surroundings and how the circumstances look. All things are possible with God, but without faith, it is impossible. That's faith!

When we have this kind of faith, all fear is gone. Why? Fear or doubt and faith cannot reside in the same heart, mind, and mouth.

Prayer:

Heavenly Father, thank You for sending Your Son Jesus Christ, as an ultimate example of how I should respond to Your love. Help me, Lord, to rest in knowing that all the plans You have for me will get completed as long as I move forward with You and keep a mustard seed faith in You.

In Jesus Name, Amen!

Chapter 4

Your Response To God's Love

Your Response To God's Love

*But maybe you don't want to serve the Lord. You must choose for
yourselves today. Today you must decide who you will serve. Will you
serve the gods that your ancestors worshipped when they lived on the
other side of the Euphrates River? Or will you serve the gods of the
Amorites who lived in this land? You must choose for yourselves. But
as for me and my family, we will serve the Lord.*

Joshua 24:15 ERV

If we understand all this about *God's Agape Love* for us,
then the question is, how do we respond? When someone
expresses his or her love to you, you have to choose
whether to reciprocate such love to the individual or not. If
you decide to accept the love, you, in turn, embrace it and
share that love with the person. If you decide not to
embrace the love, you, in turn, respond by extending alike
or friendship or no relationship at all with the individual. So
again, I ask the question, how do you respond to *God's
Agape Love*?

Even Jesus asked Peter three times, "Do you love Me?"
The love that Jesus had toward Peter was different than the
love that Peter had toward Jesus. There was a disconnect

between the love that Jesus had for Peter and the love Peter had for Jesus. Is there a disconnect between the love that God has for you and the love that you have for God?

God is not just someone we worship and serve. God is someone we should know, someone we should have a relationship with. Some people may say, how can you have a relationship with someone you cannot even see. How do I know that God can truly exist in my life?

Well, think of the wind. One does not see the wind, but you know that the wind exists. When you are looking outside or walking outside, and it is windy, you will see the wind's effects. You may see the leaves in the trees moving or things on the ground moving. You may also feel the effects of the wind when the wind touches your skin. That is the effect of the wind you see and feel.

This is the same when God is in your life and controlling your life. You cannot see Him, but you will see and feel the effects of God in your life. You will see and experience the favor, blessings, and the power of God moving in your life. When you pray and spend intimate time with God, you will experience His presence in your life. He will walk with you and talk with you every day if you allow Him to. The choice is yours. So, yes, you are right. You cannot see God, but you will see, feel and know the effects of God in your life.

God has chosen to love you and to love you unconditionally and sacrificially and to have you live an abundant, blessed, victorious life through Him. The songwriter says, "Love so Amazing, so divine, **_Demands my soul, my life, my all_**." Yes, demands. *God's Agape Love* **_demands_** a response from us. The word demands mean to require; to ask by authority; it means something owed. *God's Agape Love* requires that we love God with all of our soul, our life, our all. We owe this to God. No man has such love as a man lay down his life for his friends. Such Love!

The word of God says, in Luke 10:27,

"You shall love the Lord your God with all your heart, with all your soul, with all your strength, and with all your mind." - **_NJKV_**

Loving God with our heart, soul, strength and, mind tells us how we should love the Lord. Meaning, we should focus on LOVING GOD WITH EVERYTHING WE HAVE, WITH EVERY ASPECT OF OUR BEING, JUST LIKE JESUS DID!!!!

With All My Heart
Passionately

*Watch over your heart with all diligence,
For from it flow the springs of life.*
Proverbs 4:23 AMP

Our heart speaks to our emotions. Love God with all of our heart means loving God passionately, affectionately, and exclusively desiring this relationship.

As humans, in a relationship, we express emotions and feelings such as happiness, sadness, excitement, thankfulness, joy, anger, confidence, etc. God understands all our emotions and feelings. When we weep before Him, whether for joy or sorrow, He knows and provides what we need. As well as there are times we shout and rejoice with Him. We all have heard the phrase, "When I think of the goodness of God, my soul says Hallelujah!" The passion I express to my God.

Also, when you give your heart to someone, that person is placed first in your life. Loving God with all your heart means that your first love is God. My loyalty is to God. He is first in my heart and life.

> *We love Him because He first loved us.*
> ### *I John 4:19 NKJV*

One final aspect, the Word of God says, we should guard our hearts above all else. Your heart dictates the course of your life. Therefore, be careful to who you give your heart to. Be careful who and what consumes your heart. Because that is what will come forth in your actions, words, and deeds.

With All My Soul
Personally

But now, God's Message, the God who made you in the first place, Jacob, the One who got you started, Israel: "Don't be afraid, I've redeemed you. I've called your name. You're mine. When you're in over your head, I'll be there with you. When you're in rough waters, you will not go down. When you're between a rock and a hard place, it won't be a dead end- Because I am God, **YOUR PERSONAL GOD***, The Holy of Israel, your Savior. I paid a huge price for you: all of Egypt, with rich Cush and Seba thrown in! That's how much you meant to me! That's how much I love you! I'd* *sell off the whole world to get you back, trade the creation just for you."*

Isaiah 43:1-4 MSG Emphasis Added

The soul speaks of identity and gives us our personality. It makes us different than anyone else. Our likes and dislikes, fears and anxieties, communication, and lack of communication are expressed in our soul. God wants us to love Him in a personal and intimate way. To love Him deeply and to hold back nothing from Him, and to give Him our all.

You can be yourself with God. You don't have to be afraid to be yourself when you are communicating with God. You don't have to pretend when you come into God's presence. You come as you are. Remember, God knows you. He is just waiting on you to come to Him.

God tells us in His Word that He is our personal God. That is the extent of the relationship He wants to have with us. That is how intimate He wants to be with us. In return, this is how intimate we need to be with Him.

God wants us to be personal and intimate with Him. God wants to change our lives, but He can't do that until we are honest about what is inside. How can He remove fear if we won't admit to it?

With All My Strength
Expressively

For God so loved the world that
*He **GAVE**, His only begotten Son, …*
John 3:16 KJV Emphasis Added

When you love someone, you want to express it to them. You do things for them, and you buy them things, you give them gifts, all to express your love for them. God expressed His love to us that He GAVE His only Begotten Son.

From this, we see just how much God loves us. He gave the ultimate supreme sacrifice for you and me. His only Son Jesus gave His life for you and me. How much does He love you and me? He stretched out His arms so wide, and He said, "This is how much." Talking about loving with all of one's strength, expressively. Jesus loved you and me to death, the death of the cross.

With All My Mind
Intelligently

Your Word I have hidden in my heart,
that I might not sin against You.

Psalms 119:11 NKJV

Finally, we should love the Lord intellectually. This will keep us balanced and not be too emotional. With all my mind means to love the Lord God with and knowing the truth of His Word.

The more we study, not read, but study the Word of God, the more we will understand and appreciate our relationship with Him. Build an altar and spend time with the Lord in prayer and study the Word of God.

We are to love Him with ALL – our heart, soul, strength, and mind. We are to love God passionately, personally, expressively, and intellectually. I think Jesus is also telling us that until you love God as you should, you will never love yourself as you should. But once you do, then you can walk in confidence and not fear!!!

So how are you responding to God's Message of Love?
How are you going to respond to *God's Agape Love?*

Prayer:

Heavenly Father, thank You for showing me such incredible love. Forgive me for not loving and cherishing You as I should. I promise from this day forward, I will love You with all of my heart, my soul, my strength, and my mind.

In Jesus Name, Amen!

Chapter 5

A Transformed Life

A Transformed Life

When I was a child, I talked like a child, I thought like a child, and I made plans like a child. When I became a man, I stopped those childish ways. It is the same with us. Now we see God as if we are looking at a reflection in a mirror. But then, in the future, we will see him right before our eyes. Now I know only a part, but at that time I will know fully, as God has known me. So these three things continue: faith, hope, and love. And the greatest of these is love.
1 Corinthians 13:11-13 ERV

In 1 Corinthians 13, when Paul was talking to Corinthian's church about *God's Agape Love,* he said that this *Agape Love* is more than just following Jesus to be connected to God. He said that this, *God Agape Love,* transforms us to be the people God created us to be. In essence, *God's Agape Love* is a transformational love. This means *God's Agape Love* is a love that changes you.

In the KJV Dictionary, it states that transformation, in theology, is "a change of heart in man, by which his disposition and temper are conformed to the divine image; a change from enmity to holiness and love." This means a change in one's heart resulting in one's natural disposition and temper changing. When you talk about one's natural disposition and temper, it means a change in a person's state of mind-- a change in a person's thinking. Hence, *God's Agape Love* changes one from within! Change into the image of God; transform to holiness and love.

The Butterfly

For a butterfly to become a butterfly, it has to go through a process called metamorphosis. Metamorphosis in Greek means transformation. This process requires four stages, the egg, larva, pupa, and adult. It begins as an egg laid on plants by an adult. The next stage is the larva, and the larva becomes a caterpillar. A fully-grown caterpillar is a pupa protected in the cocoon, and out from that cocoon comes a beautiful butterfly. However, while in the cocoon, it first goes through an inward change followed by an outward change. This is the change that needs to happen to us.

Listen, anything worth striving for is not easy. Rest assured that this transformation involves a struggle. The butterfly does not start as a butterfly but goes through stages. Once the caterpillar is in a cocoon, it then fights and struggles to get out. But just like that butterfly, it is not an easy task to transform our thinking, and it involves some struggle. It involves work and effort on our part.

Something important to know. If you clip open the cocoon, the butterfly will not fly. If you help in the process of trying to make it easy for the butterfly, it stunts the butterfly and it comes out crippled, and unable to fly. The caterpillar must go through the process to become the butterfly. We have to go through a process to get to the place where God wants us to be.

The process is that we need to go through an inward change, and then comes the outward change. The inward change is the change of mindset; then comes the outward change, which is the change in our speech, attitude, actions, and form. When we start to get that mindset of Christ, there is nothing that will stop us. We will begin to walk in boldness and confidence and no more fear.

Change Your Thinking

So I beg you, brothers and sisters, because of the great mercy God has shown us, offer your lives as a living sacrifice to Him- an offering that is only for God and pleasing to Him. Considering what He has done, it is only right that you should worship Him in this way. Don't change yourselves to be like the people of this world, __but let God change you inside with a new way of thinking. Then you will be able to understand and accept what God wants for you.__ *You will be able to know what is good and pleasing to Him and what is perfect.*

Romans 12:1-2 ERV Emphasis Added

Once we accept *God's Agape Love* into our lives, then we need to begin changing into the image of God. Since God has demonstrated to us such a great love, we, in turn, should offer ourselves completely to Him. Dedicating all of ourselves only to Him and pleasing to Him. Accordingly, the Word of God tells us that we have to be transformed by renewing our minds. We have to let God change us inside with a new way of thinking. We have to have a mindset change. Thus, to dispel fear and walk in boldness, we need to allow the Lord to renew our minds, daily. Once our minds are renewed in Christ, we will have a new way of thinking; a Christ-like way of thinking.

In your life together, **think the way Christ Jesus thought.**
Philippians 2:5 ERV Emphasis Added

Let God direct your thoughts, actions, assignments, and lives. Once your thinking changes, your thoughts change, your words change, your actions change, and ultimately your life changes. It's a process.

The scripture says in Romans 12:1-2, do not change to be like the people of the world. Do not conform to the world. We should not allow the ways of the world and the customs of the world to dictate to us.

The word "conform" in the KJV Dictionary states, "to comply with or yield to; to live or act according to; as, to conform to the fashion or to custom." To comply or yield means to listen to and do the world's ways, to think like the world. The world's ways is control by the prince of the world, who is Satan, our adversary. We should not act or live according to the ways of our adversary. NO! That would be living a life of fear, doubt, timidity, lack, and cowardice. In living that diabolical life, we are walking in constant defeat.

> *The thief (**our adversary**) comes only in order to steal and kill and destroy (**you**)."*
> **John 10:10(a) AMP Emphasis Added**

That is not the life that God has for us! God wants us to live a life that is full and overflowing in the abundance of victory. Thus, we have to change to live according to the Word of God. Yes, I said, have to. We must change our thinking, and therefore, we will begin to think like God. I have seen relationships where one spouse knows what the other is thinking and can thus complete their sentences. How? They know the person extremely well. We need to know God, like this. How? We must spend time with Him in prayer and study His Word.

When we know God, we know He means no Fear!!! The world, controlled by Satan, wants to put fear and doubt into us. To make you feel as though you cannot achieve and that you are not good enough. To make you think that you were not meant to do the extraordinary. That thinking is so contrary to our God and His Word.

I can do all things [which He has called me to do] through Him who strengthens and empowers me [to fulfill His purpose-I am self-sufficient in Christ's sufficiency; I am ready for anything and equal to anything through Him who infuses me with inner strength and confident peace.]

Philippians 4:13 AMP

The Word of God tells you that you can achieve and accomplish anything and everything that God has called you to do. You are empowered to do; you are equipped to do, you are self-sufficient in Christ's sufficiency. Consequently, be ready for anything and everything through Jesus Christ.

You see, in changing our thinking and mindset, we will act and perform differently and without fear. And once this happens, you will understand and know what God has in store for you. God has embedded in you all the gifts and skills you need to be successful. Have you tapped into them as yet? You can only answer this in the affirmative if you have begun to change if you have begun to perfect *God's Agape Love* in you. Have you?

Listen, as your thinking, attitude, speech, and actions change, your demeanor and outward being will change.

Then you will find yourself walking in such boldness and confidence. Then you find yourself walking in the same power that transformed Jesus on the Mount of Transfiguration.

> *"He was transfigured before them. His*
> *face shone like the sun, and His*
> *clothes became as white as the light."*
> ### Matthew 17:2 NKJV.

Our minds contain great power. We all know that the Spiritual Battlefield is in the mind. That is where the devil attacks us – in the mind. The devil, our adversary, will do everything possible to get us to believe his lies and stop us from achieving our purpose and goals.

If the devil can get us to think his way – he will.

If the devil can get us to believe a lie – he will.

If the devil can get us to become confused – he will.

If the devil can get us to doubt God – he will.

If the devil can make us think we can't – he will

If the devil can make us think we are not good enough – he will

If the devil can get us to become fearful – he will.

The only power the devil has over us is the power we allow him to have over us.

So submit to [the authority of] God. Resist the devil [stand firm against him] and he will flee from you.

James 4:7 AMP

The devil has no place in your mind, your thinking, and your life. We need to allow God to change our thinking, and then we can live the lives that our Heavenly Father has planned for us.

Prayer

Heavenly Father, change me. Lord, I am ready to think differently and move forward in the life You have for me with the guidance and leading of the Holy Spirit. Change my thinking, my mindset, to be transformed into your thinking.

In Jesus Name, Amen!

Chapter 6

Change Your Words
What Are You Speaking?

Change Your Words
What Are You Speaking?

"Let me tell you something: Every one of these careless words is going to come back to haunt you. There will be a time of Reckoning. Words are powerful; take them seriously. Words can be your salvation. Words can also be your damnation."

Matthew 12:36-37 MSG

What are you speaking? Think about this, the Book of Proverbs tells us that Life and Death are in the power of the tongue. God tells us that His words never return void but accomplishes everything that it sets out to accomplish.

In the same way, my words leave my mouth,
and they don't come back without results.
My words make the things happen that I want to happen. They
succeed in doing what I
send them to do.

Isaiah 55:11 ERV

Does it matter what we say? Does it matter how we speak about and to a situation or our lives? Absolutely! If I speak fear instead of boldness and confidence, I will be fearful. If I speak sickness and death instead of life and wholeness, I will be ill and die. If I speak sadness instead of joy, I will be unhappy. If I speak defeat instead of victory, I will fail. Evaluate your life and how you speak and ask yourself, what am I speaking? What am I saying?

Words are so important and carry so much weight and power. The words we speak are essential to our lives and crucial to our outcome. Words bring about change in our life. Words set the direction of our life. Words affect. They can be a blessing or a curse. Words can destroy and tear down, but words can also build up and conqueror. Words can bring fear and distress, but words can also bring confidence and boldness. Words can bring curses and sickness, but words can also bring blessings and healing. Words matter. So we must consider and be aware of what we say. As a result, we ought to learn to speak words of faith, confidence, boldness, positiveness, life, and hope.

Proverbs summarize it this way:

Your words can be as satisfying as fruit, as pleasing as the food that fills your stomach. The tongue can speak words that brings life or death. Those who love to talk must be ready to accept what it brings.

Proverbs 18:20-21

We absolutely must examine the words coming forth from our mouth. We must daily listen to what our tongue is confessing. You and I have the power to bring good or bad, positive or negative, boldness or fear upon ourselves, in our lives, and to others. We eat the fruit of what we say.

Our words can trap us:

If you have been snared with the words of your lips, If you have been trapped by the speech of your mouth.

Proverbs 6:2 AMP

Our words can bring anger or peace:

A soft and gentle and thoughtful answer turns away wrath, But harsh and painful and careless words stir up anger.

Proverbs 15:1 AMP

Our words can build up and encourage as well as crush

72

and break the spirit:

A soothing tongue [speaking words that build up and encourage] is a tree of life, but a perverse tongue [speaking words that overwhelm and depress] crushes the spirit.

Proverbs 15:4 AMP

Our words can be wise or foolish:

The tongue of the wise speaks knowledge that is pleasing and acceptable, but the [babbling] mouth of fools spouts folly.

Proverbs 15:2 AMP

Our words can bring healing:

Pleasant words are like a honeycomb, sweet and delightful to the soul and healing to the body.

Proverbs 16:24 AMP

There is one who speaks rashly like the thrusts of a sword, but the tongue of the wise brings healing.

Proverbs 12:18 AMP

Our words are life-giving:

The words of a man's mouth are like deep waters [copious and difficult to fathom]; The fountain of [mature, godly] wisdom is like a bubbling stream [sparkling, fresh, pure, and life-giving].

73

Proverbs 18:4 AMP

Your words are powerful! The Lord has promised tremendous amounts of blessings in our life through the Word of God. So acknowledge that I am going to confess and speak the Word of God over myself as of today. Remember, we eat the fruit of what we say.

If you want to accomplish everything that God has already appointed for you, then change your words. You remember Jeremiah and Moses. When God told them their assignment, both men basically told God they could not do it and gave God all sought of excuses. Both Moses and Jeremiah were fearful of doing the assignment that God had given them. Doesn't this sound like us when God reveals to us His assignment for our lives? We need to check the words coming out of our mouth. Do not say, "I can't" to the Lord. As a matter of fact, take some words and phrases out of your vocabulary – like No, I can't, I am not good enough, I'm scared. Words do matter!!!

Unfortunately, we fail to realize how significant our speech really is. And so, over and over and over again, we speak words that bring ill health, death, and destruction. And then we wonder why we are depressed and hurting and why we are in the situation and predicament we are in.

We need to release words of faith and not fear. That is the power of words. When fear wants to grip you, speak words of power and faith and achieve positive results. God's words will produce exactly what He says. Be wise and careful what words you are placing in the atmosphere.

If you and I were to change the way we view our mouths and recognize the power of our words, we could literally change our entire atmosphere for good. Ask yourself, am I bringing favor and blessings into this situation, or am I bringing a curse? Am I walking in fear, or am I walking in boldness and confidence? Do you need to alter your speech accordingly to invite life, favor, and blessings into your atmosphere? If we allow change to come to our thinking and speaking, we can accomplish the impossible.

Prayer:

Heavenly Father, I yield my tongue and words to You. Help me to speak words that bring life, healing, power and victory to my situations, circumstances, to my life, and to those whom I love.

In Jesus Name, Amen!

Chapter 7

Dispel Fear & Walk In Boldness

Dispel Fear & Walk In Boldness

But now, thus says the LORD, who created you, O Jacob, And He who formed you, O Israel: "Fear not, for I have redeemed you; I have called you by your name; You are Mine.

Isaiah 43:1 NKJV

We walk around in fear believing that we are not capable of accomplishing great things in our lives. I can't start and own a Fortune 500 company. I can't be the next Pulitzer Prize inventor. I can't minister to hundreds of thousands of people. I can't own my own business with 300 employees. I can't be an author of many successful books. I can't own many real estate properties. I can't be a millionaire. I can't; I can't; I can't.

One day, a husband and wife, both of who are singers, were practicing a song. Since I am singing the melody, the husband said you should sing the alto like this, and he demonstrated to her what to sing. The wife immediately said I can't, and her husband said, stop saying you can't and listen. She listened, and what happened? She realized that she was able to sing the alto part. The best aspect of this is that it sounded so beautiful, and the words of the song, coupled with their voices, blessed so many people.

What is FEAR? According to the Merriam-Webster Dictionary, one of the definitions for the word "Fear" is "an unpleasant often, strong emotion caused by anticipation or awareness of danger." In the KJV Dictionary, one of the definitions of the word "Fear" is "a painful emotion or passion excited by an expectation of evil, or the apprehension of impending danger." It also says that Fear is "an uneasiness of mind, upon the thought of future evil likely to befall us." It continues to say, "To be in apprehension of evil; to be afraid; to feel anxiety on account of some expected evil; Threat of evil – whether the threat is *real or imagined*." The acronym for the word "Fear" is "False Evidence Appearing Real." Most importantly, the Word of God states,

"God has not given us a spirit of fear, but of power and of love and of a sound mind."
2 Timothy 1:7 NKJV

From the scripture and the definitions, we see that fear is a spirit that comes upon you, resulting in a state of mind. It is a strong feeling and painful emotion that deposits an uneasiness of the mind. It stems from evil, real or imagined, and it makes one feel inadequate to accomplish something; to achieve because the individual believes something that is not there. It will trap you in life that you will not progress and move forward as you should. It is a slow death from an abundant life.

Throughout the Bible, we see that God gives His people commands, an authoritative order, on what He wants His people to do. One of the most often repeated commands in the Word of God is "Do Not Fear," "Fear Not," or "Don't Be Afraid." Theologians say that these phrases are stated over 365 times in the bible. If these phrases are stated so many times in the Word of God, What is God telling us? Even though this spirit of fear may try to overtake your mind, don't allow it. Do not allow fear to dictate and control your life because there is no reason to fear when you are in Me.

In the Book of Timothy, the Apostle Paul was writing to Timothy, as Timothy was Paul's younger protégé and a pastor in Ephesus' church. The Apostle Paul was giving Timothy words of encouragement since Timothy was battling with the spirit of fear. Timothy had a timid personality, and the Apostle Paul was encouraging him to preach and teach the truth of the gospel with boldness. Yes, God can use anyone to accomplish what He wants to, even a shy, timid man or woman to preach and teach the gospel of Jesus Christ. Why? Because God knows the boldness and the gifts that He has embedded in that individual. How many of us can relate to this? I can! Walking around with a timid, shy and fearful spirit and thus, not walking in boldness, missing out on so much in life. Remember, the gifts that God has given us should be used in boldness and not in fear.

So the Apostle Paul was reminding Timothy that when it comes to preaching and teaching the gospel, the gift that God has given him, he should do it with courage and boldness.

"God doesn't want us to be shy with His gifts, but bold and loving and sensible."

2 Timothy 1:7 MSG

And very importantly, the Apostle Paul was telling Timothy that the spirit of fear that he is experiencing does not come from God.

The word "fear" in Greek means cowardice or timidity, and these character traits do not describe God in any way. God has not given us the spirit of fear, cowardice, or timidity. God is not timid, cowardly, shy, fearful, afraid, nervous, or worried about anything, and because you have the Spirit of God, the *Agape Love* of God, living inside of you, neither should you. The scripture does tell us that God has given us the spirit of power, love, sound judgment, and personal discipline. God has given us the power and the ability that results in a calm, well-balanced mind and self-control.

"For God did not give us a spirit of timidity or cowardice or fear, but [He has given us a spirit] of power and of love and of sound judgment and personal discipline [abilities that result in a calm, well-balanced mind and self-control]."

2 Timothy 1:7 AMP

As believers walking in fear, there is an internal struggle happening. Timothy was experiencing this. One cannot focus on your abilities or on thinking whether you can accomplish what God has set out for you to do. Instead, be filled with the Spirit of God, *the Holy Spirit*, walk in the *Agape Love* of God, and then you will overcome the spirit of fear because your thinking, attitude, speech, and actions change.

But you will receive power and ability when the Holy Spirit comes upon you; and you will be My witnesses [to tell people about Me] both in Jerusalem and in all Judea, and Samaria, and even to the ends of the earth."

Acts 1:8 AMP

God has blessed and given all of us gifts and abilities to accomplish specific assignment(s). We have to recognize and draw from what God has placed in us without fear. If the spirit of fear does not come from God, then there is only one other source it comes from. Fear is a spirit that the adversary wants to put on you. He wants you to feel that you cannot accomplish or utilize the gifts, talents, and abilities that God has placed in you.

People say to me, Denise, do not be afraid or do not let fear overtake you. To myself, I would say easier said than done. How can I do that? Let me share some of the actions I have and will continue to take that has aided me in overcoming fear.

First, I had to realize and know whom I serve and who I am to Him. I love and serve the King of Kings and Lord of Lords. There is no one greater than Him. He never leaves me. He is with me 24/7, even when I think He is not. He supplies my every need. When I need picking up, He does that. When I need a hug, He gives it to me. When I need a push, trust me, He pushes me to do. My God has all power, and that same power, the power of the Holy Spirit, is living and abiding within me. So I walk my life in this power. Thank God for the Holy Spirit! Walking in this power, I had to change my mindset and how I spoke. I had to think better of myself. I had to think of faith and powerful thoughts. I also had to stop saying "No" all the time and venture out into the deep with God. If I have the Supreme Being backing me up, why do I fear? I have no reason to!

Next, I learned that I have to renounce that spirit of fear when Satan tries to put it on me and declare the spirit of boldness over myself. I will say, Lord, Your Word says that what we bind in earth shall be bound in heaven and what we loose in earth shall be loose in heaven. So I bind the spirit of fear, timidity, and shyness over me right now. I bind up every root of fear, unbelief, and doubt in Jesus' Name. And I loose the spirit of boldness, confidence, fearlessness, soberness, and healing of my mind in Jesus' Name Amen!

At times I would have to say to myself that I will do this no matter what. Holy Spirit, help me to get this done. Then I would do it. Once you step out and do it, watch what happens. You build up confidence, trust, and faith in God working through you. Why do you think that Satan wants you to be fearful? Because He knows the potential and the gifts, talents, and abilities that God has placed in you, and he does not want you to succeed. Stop letting him win. You need to realize the gifts, talents and abilities that God has placed in you. We are more than conquerors. You are more than a conqueror!!!

We have to put our trust and faith in God and rely on Him. I talk to God all the time. Before I give a word, I say to the Holy Spirit, ok, You lead, and I will follow. Currently, I have projects that the Lord has instructed me to work on. I first wanted to say to Him, who me? But then I stopped myself and said, yes Lord. Let's go. You will be amazed by what God will do through you.

Finally, I will utilize the "Power of the Nevertheless:"

The Power of The Nevertheless

So it was, as the multitude pressed about Him to hear the word of God, that He stood by the Lake of Gennesaret, and saw two boats standing by the lake; but the fishermen had gone from them and were washing their nets. Then He got into one of the boats, which was Simon's, and asked him to put out a little from the land. And He sat down and taught the multitudes from the boat. When He had stopped speaking, He said to Simon, "Launch out into the deep and let down your nets for a catch." But Simon answered and said to Him, "Master, we have toiled all night and caught nothing; nevertheless at Your word I will let down the net." And when they had done this, they caught a great number of fish, and their net was breaking. So they signaled to their partners in the other boat to come and help them. And they came and filled both the boats, so that they began to sink. When Simon Peter saw it, he fell down at Jesus' knees, saying, "Depart from me, for I am a sinful man, O Lord!" For he and all who were with him were astonished at the catch of fish which they had taken; and so also were James and John, the sons of Zebedee, who were partners with Simon. And Jesus said to Simon, "Do not be afraid. From now on you will catch men." So when they had brought their boats to land, they forsook all and followed Him.

Luke 5:1-11 NKJV

The aspect of this story that I love is that one word changed the outcome of one's life. That word is "Nevertheless." From Thayer's Greek Lexicon Abridged, in the New Testament Greek, it states that the word "nevertheless" is used "after negative sentences" and "serves to mark a transition to something new." Meaning changing something negative into something positive. The Merriam-Webster Dictionary states that nevertheless means, "In spite of all that: However."

In the scripture, we see that Jesus tells Simon Peter to "Launch out into the deep and let down your nets for a catch." Do you really think that Simon Peter wanted to throw his net out again? Think about it, he had just toiled all night, and he had cleaned up his fishing gear, and the Lord is telling him to go back out there. Simon Peter was a fisherman, so he knew when he should be fishing and when not. That is why he said to Jesus, "Master, we have toiled all night and caught nothing." But Simon Peter put his trust and faith in his Lord and said, "nevertheless at *Your Word* I will let down the net." The moment Simon Peter let down the net, the overflow began to happen, and they caught so much fish that their nets began to break that they need the assistance of their partners to help them.

What am I saying here? Just like Simon Peter used the power of the nevertheless, you can too. When Satan tries to throw that spirit of fear on you, stand bold and say, Nevertheless of your tricks, manipulations, lies, and deceptions, Satan, I believe the Word of the Lord.

"God has not given us a spirit of fear, but of power and of love and of a sound mind."
2 Timothy 1:7 NKJV

I can do all things through Christ who strengthens me.
Philippians 4:13 NKJV

While I was in Law School, I had to hold on to Philippians 4:13. I often believed that I could not make it through and that I was not capable of reaching this achievement. Constantly, I had to repeat that scripture and tell myself that I can do this and that I am going to make it through.

At some point in life, all of us have faced and had to overcome the spirit of fear. It may be worrying about provision or protection.

> *Give all your worries to Him (Jesus),*
> *because He cares for you.*
> ### 1 Peter 5:7 ERV Emphasis Added

You may worry about what other people may say, think or do. Sometimes you have to not listen to people. Some people in your life may not want to see you move forward, or they want you to move forward but just enough to stay connected to them. You may declare to yourself that you do not have the ability to accomplish a particular goal. Open your mind to God and ask the Lord to give you the strength, the power, the boldness, the confidence to move forward in His plans for you. Focus on God, learn to lean on God, and trust Him. God is saying, do not fear! Remember that FEAR is False Evidence Appearing Real – Do not tell yourself things that are not there. Change your thinking; I had to change my mindset. Change how you speak; I had to. Listen, it is time for a change! Begin to experience the magnitude of our God.

Prayer:

Lord, I know that You have not given me the spirit of fear but of love, power, and a sound mind. Therefore, I renounce the spirit of fear, cowardice, and timidity over my life and mind. I declare and decree that I will walk in Your boldness and confidence, for You have given me the spirit of love, power and a sound mind from this day forward. I will think and speak words of faith, life, positiveness, and hope. My trust and faith are in You Lord and You alone.

In Jesus Name, Amen!

Chapter 8

The Magnitude Of Our God

The Magnitude Of Our God

Jeremiah, I am the Lord. I am the God of every person on the earth. You know that nothing is impossible for me.

Jeremiah 32:27 ERV

God is the God of the impossible! Expect God to surprise you and to do the unthinkable, and to pull off the unexpected! GOD CAN DO IT! Ephesians 3:20-21 says,

"With God's power working in us, He can do much, much more than anything we can ask or think of. To Him be glory in the church and in Christ Jesus for all time, forever and ever. Amen.

ERV

Our God is the Almighty God! His power and ability are limitless, and there is nothing He cannot do. To the extent to which we experience His power and ability in our lives depends entirely upon us. We serve a God who is infinite. He is all-powerful, all-knowing, and all-present. God is completely capable, period. He is a God whose power, ability, and love knows no limits. Yet, even though we know this and continually say it, we tend to limit the power of God. By limiting God, we are putting God in a box. God loves us so much that He has already embedded in us everything we need to be successful, prosperous, and victorious. We have no reason to fear or doubt the love of God because God is greater. You may say greater than what? Than anything!!!

God is greater than the prison we put around our minds. God is greater than any inadequacies we may think we have. God is greater than any obstacle we may face. God is greater than any barrier set before us. God is greater than the norm. God is greater than the earthly economy. GOD IS GREATER!

God Is Greater Than Imprisonment

Have you ever felt imprisoned, mentally, emotionally, or spiritually, feeling that there is just no way out? Perhaps you are imprisoned by your thinking, which stuns us from accomplishing so much. You feel that you are not capable of doing a particular task and so fear overtakes you. You feel that if you attempt to do it, you will fail. You are mentally imprisoned from living the victorious life that God has promised to you.

The Book of Acts Chapter 16 tells us the story of how Paul and Silas were imprisoned. The Roman citizens rose against Paul and Silas and presented them to their Rulers. They tore their clothes and severely beat them, and threw them in prison. The jailor was paid to keep watch over Paul and Silas in prison and make sure that Paul and Silas do not escape. To accomplish this, the jailor placed Paul and Silas far inside the jail and put Paul and Silas's feet in secured firm stocks. They were imprisoned, they could not move, and they could not escape. In their own strength, Paul and Silas were powerless to change the situation. They had no way out.

Despite their imprisonment, Paul and Silas began to pray and sing worship songs to God. They might have been physically imprisoned, but spiritually they kept their eyes on their Lord. So what happened? Suddenly, the jail foundation began to shake at midnight, and all the doors of the jail opened. And the chains of all the prisoners fell off.

Although Paul and Silas were in a difficult predicament, being severely beaten and facing death, neither of them feared the unknown and neither allowed fear to grip them. They may have been imprisoned physically but not mentally. Instead they rested in their God by praying and worshipping their God. They knew that only God could change and have them work through this situation and be victorious.

In life, do not allow Satan to imprison you by making you think that you are not capable. Do not allow fear to consume you that you become mentally imprisoned. Instead, when this feeling and mindset begins to take hold of you, talk to God and worship Him. Focus on worshipping the Lord and watch your mindset change. Watch the chains of imprisonment fall off of your mind and thinking. Watch the power of God overtake you. Your mindset becomes stronger and fixed on the God of the impossible.

God Is Greater Than Inadequacies

At times you may feel that you are inadequate to accomplish a particular assignment of the Lord. Per the Merriam-Webster Dictionary, the word inadequate means: not adequate, not enough or good; insufficient; not capable. At times you may feel that you are inadequate. Every time you feel this, you say to God that He made you insufficient, not good enough, and incapable of accomplishing and living the life God has in store for you.

Remember Moses. In Exodus chapter 3, Moses had an experience with the burning bush. God appeared to Moses through the burning bush and told Moses to take off his sandals because he was standing on Holy Ground. God and Moses proceeded to have a conversation regarding Israel. God told Moses that He had seen His people's troubles in Egypt and that He has heard their cries. Consequently, He told Moses that He is going to save His people and deliver them from bondage through Moses.

Moses believed that he was inadequate to accomplish

this. He told God that he was not a great man; he was not a good speaker, and God, can you send someone else? But God, as always, knows better. God had placed everything into Moses from birth that he needed to accomplish this assignment from the Lord. The end result, the people of Israel were saved and delivered from Egypt. They were set free from bondage by God using Moses.

Let's not forget Jeremiah. God chose Jeremiah to be a prophet to the nations. As a matter of fact, God told Jeremiah that He chose him to do this before he was born. Jeremiah, on the other hand, told God that he was inadequate to do that. He said, Lord, I do not know how to speak, and I am just a child. God had to tell Jeremiah do not say that and do not be afraid. You must do as I instruct, go where I tell you to go, say what I want you to say. Further, the Lord said, I will be with you always.

Both of these men felt inadequate at first. Once Jeremiah and Moses released their fear and allowed God to use them, they accomplished the assignment(s) God had for them. Fear can make one feel in adequate to do. Do not ever feel as though you are inadequate to accomplish anything.

> *I praise You, for I am fearfully and*
> *wonderfully made; Marvelous are*
> *Your works, And that my*
> *soul knows very well.*

Psalms 139:14 NKJV

Be secure in knowing that God is with you and that God has equipped you with everything you need to succeed and be victorious.

God Is Greater Than Obstacles

Sometimes we experience obstacles, blockages that hinder us from moving forward or progressing. Then fear sets in because we automatically think, oh God does not want me to do this, or this is just too difficult. Remember, Fear is False Evidence Appearing Real.

We all know the famous story of David and Goliath. The Philistines gathered an army against Saul and the Israelite soldiers. For forty days, the Philistines' prizefighter,

Goliath, challenged the Israelite soldiers to have one of their soldiers fight him. But Saul and the Israelite soldiers felt that the Philistines were an obstacle for them moving forward, and they were extremely afraid because Goliath was 9 feet tall, and they knew that it was impossible for them to beat him.

Here comes David, who was just a young boy that was sent to the battleground to deliver some supplies but, more importantly to see how his brothers were doing. The moment David arrives, both sides are lined up for war, and as always, Goliath shouted things against Israel. Fear sets in again, and the Israelite soldiers run away. But David had no fear. He wanted to know who this Goliath was and why he thinks he can talk against the army of the living God. David had a different mindset than the Israelite soldiers. Ultimately, David tells Saul that the people should not let Goliath discourage them; he will fight Goliath. Saul said, you, David, you are not even a soldier, and Goliath has been a soldier since he was a boy.

David, knowing who his God is, not limiting his God,

and therefore not fearing, said I had killed a lion, and a bear and I will kill Goliath because Goliath has made fun of the army of the Living God! Sure enough, David slays Goliath through the power of the Almighty God. Did David have fear? No!

David was facing the same situation as the Israelite soldiers, David did not fear. He trusted and rested in the God he served. The obstacle was not an obstacle at all. God is much bigger!

God Is Greater Than The Norm

When Abraham was 100 years old, God told him that He would give Sarah, Abraham's wife, a child. Abraham said God, I am 100 years old, and Sarah is 90 years old. She cannot have a child. Right there, Abraham limited the power and ability of God. God said, I am going to give you a son, and He did. Was this the norm for a man, who is 100, and a woman who was well past childbearing age to have a child? No, but our God is limitless!

How many times does God tell us that He will do something against the norm in our lives, yet we cannot believe it, simply because it is not the norm. We do not serve the God of the norm, but we serve the God of the impossible.

The Lord says, "My thoughts are not like yours, your ways are not like mine. Just as the heavens are higher than the earth, so My ways are higher than your ways, and My thoughts are higher than your thoughts. "Rain and snow fall from the sky and don't return until they have watered the ground. Then the ground causes the plants to sprout and grow, and they produce seeds for the farmer and food for people to eat. In the same way, My words leave My mouth, and they don't come back without results. My words make the things happen that I want to happen. They succeed in doing what I send them to do.

Isaiah 55:8-11 ERV

Prayer:

Heavenly Father, I realize that You are so powerful and mighty. There is nothing too hard for You. Help me always to realize that I serve and love the God of the Impossible.

In Jesus Name, Amen!

Chapter 9

A New Beginning

A New Beginning

Let's do a self-evaluation. Look to see where you were 5 years ago or even 2 years ago and where you are now. If nothing has changed in your life with Christ, if nothing has changed for the positive as far as accomplishments, something needs to be revamped. If your relationship with the Lord is the same – you need a change. If you say and do the same things repeatedly and no progress – you need to halt and do a 180-degree turn. Wake-up, you are like that hamster in the wheel spinning round and round and heading nowhere. Do not wait any longer. Begin now to change. Change is here! Start achieving and accomplishing. Are you ready? Get going!

Today, make a declaration to yourself that you will not be fearful from this day forward but that you will walk in the confidence and boldness of your God and achieve the assignment(s) and task(s) that God has placed before you. There are more than ninety scriptures and quotes encouraging and inspiring you to overcome fear and walk in a different mind-set in this chapter. Over the next 3 months, take a scripture or quote each day and meditate on it to enlighten you through the day. Let this be a new beginning for you.

Scriptures

Where God's love is, there is no fear, because God's perfect love takes away fear. It is His punishment that makes a person fear. So His love is not made perfect in the one who has fear.

1 John 4:18 ERV

Don't panic. I'm with you. There's no need to fear for I'm your God. I'll give you strength. I'll help you. I'll hold you steady, keep a firm grip on you.

Isaiah 41:10 MSG

Don't worry about anything, but pray and ask God for everything you need, always giving thanks for what you have. And because you belong to Christ Jesus, God's peace will stand guard over all your thoughts and feelings. His peace can do this far better than our human minds.

Philippians 4:6-7 ERV

But now, thus says the Lord,…Fear not, for I have redeemed you; I have called you by your name; you are mine.

Isaiah 43:1 NKJV

The Spirit God gave us does not make us afraid. His Spirit is a source of power and love and self-control.

2 Timothy 1:7 ERV

Yet in all these things we are more than conquerors through Him who loved us.

Romans 8:37 NKJV

Remember, I commanded you to be strong and brave. Don't be afraid, because the Lord your God will be with you wherever you go.

Joshua 1:9 ERV

Yes, I am sure that nothing can separate us from God's love-not death, life, angels, or ruling spirits. I am sure that nothing now, nothing in the future, no powers, nothing above us or nothing below us-nothing in the whole created world-will ever be able to separate us from the love God has shown us in Christ Jesus our Lord.

Romans 8:38-39 ERV

Whenever I am afraid, I will trust in You.

Psalms 56:3 NJKV

Jesus said.....Don't be afraid; just believe.

Mark 5:36 ERV

Say to those who are fearful-hearted, "Be strong, do not fear! Behold, your God will come..."

Isaiah 35:4 NKJV

The Lord is with me, so I will not be afraid. No one on

earth can do anything to harm me. The Lord is my helper. I will see my enemies defeated.

Psalms 118:6-7 ERV

Even though I walk through the [sunless] valley of the shadow of death, I fear no evil, for You are with me; Your rod [to protect] and Your staff [to guide], they comfort and console me.

Psalms 23:4 AMP

The Lord's angel builds a camp around His followers, and He protects them.

Psalms 24:7 ERV

You must not fear them, for the Lord your God Himself fights for you.

Deuteronomy 3:22 NKJV

I went to the Lord for help, and He listened. He saved me from all that I fear.

Psalms 34:4 ERV

I leave you peace. It is my own peace I give you. I give you peace in a different way than the world does. So don't be troubled. Don't be afraid.

John 14:27 ERV

So don't worry about tomorrow. Each day has enough

trouble of its own. Tomorrow will have its own worries.

Matthew 6:34 ERV

In the multitude of my anxieties within me, Your comforts delight my soul.

Psalms 94:19 NKJV

God is our protection and source of strength. He is always ready to help us in times of trouble.

Psalms 46:1 ERV

Anxiety in a man's heart weighs it down, But a good (encouraging) word makes it glad.

Proverbs 12:25 AMP

Jesus stood up and gave a command to the wind and the water. He said, "Quiet! Be still!" Then the wind stopped, and the lake became calm. He said to His followers, "Why are you afraid? Do you still have no faith?"

Mark 4:39-40 ERV

But immediately He talked with them and said to them, "Be of good cheer! It is I; do not be afraid."

Mark 6:50 NKJV

Therefore humble yourselves under the mighty hand of God, that He may exalt you in due time, casting all your care upon Him, for He cares for you.

1 Peter 5:6-7 NKJV

I am the Lord your God, who holds your right hand. And I tell you, "Don't be afraid! I will help you."
Isaiah 41:13 ERV

Give all your worries to Him, because He cares for you.
1 Peter 5:7 ERV

Lord, You are my Light and my Savior, so why should I be afraid of anyone? The Lord is where my life is safe, so I will be afraid of no one!
Psalms 27:1 ERV

Be strong and be brave. Don't be afraid of those people because the Lord your God is with you. He will not fail you or leave you.
Deuteronomy 31:6 ERV

Give your worries to the Lord, and He will care for you. He will never let those who are good be defeated.
Psalms 55:22 ERV

Fear can be a trap, but if you trust in the Lord, you will be safe.
Proverbs 29:25 ERV

He put his right hand on me and said, "Don't be afraid! I am the First and the Last."- **Revelation 1:17 ERV**

Quotes

Faith is Birth, Fear is Taught.

Dr. Kevin A. Williams

Courage is the power of the mind to overcome fear.

Martin Luther King, Jr.

When Fear Knocks On Your Door Send FAITH To Answer.

Joyce Meyer

Feed your faith and your fears will starve to death.

Unknown

Change your mind, change your outcome.

Dr. Kevin A. Williams

Faith is taking the first step even when you don't see the whole staircase.

Martin Luther King, Jr.

"I learned that courage was not the absence of fear, but the triumph over it. The brave man is not he who does not feel afraid, but he who conquers fear."

Nelson Mandela

Nothing in life is to be feared. It is only to be understood. Now is the time to understand more, so that we may fear less.

Marie Curie

You can't make decisions based on fear and the possibility of what might happen.

Michelle Obama

Decide that you want it more than you are afraid of it.

Bill Cosby

The key to change…is to let go of fear.

Roseanne Cash

One of the greatest discoveries a man makes, one of his great surprises, is to find he can do what he was afraid he couldn't do.

Henry Ford

Make this day your servant and not your master.

Dr. Kevin A. Williams

Don't let the fear of striking out hold you back.

Babe Ruth

Do the thing you fear and the death of fear is certain.

Ralph Waldo Emerson

Fear is only as deep as the mind allows

Japanese Proverb

Do the thing you fear to do and keep on doing…that is the quickest and surest way ever yet discovered to conquer fear.

Dale Carnegie

I have learned over the years that when one's mind is made up, this diminishes fear; knowing what must be done does away with fear.

Rosa Parks

The cave you fear to enter holds the treasure you seek.

Joseph Campbell

Remembering that I'll be dead soon is the most important tool I've ever encountered to help me make the big choices in life. Because almost everything – all external expectations, all pride, all fear of embarrassment or failure – these things just fall away in the face of death, leaving only what is truly important.

Steve Jobs

Everything you want is on the other side of fear.

Jack Canfield

The way you overcome shyness is to become so wrapped up in something that you forget to be afraid.

Lady Bird Johnson

Don't fear failure so much that you refuse to try new things. The saddest summary of a life contains three descriptions: could have, might have, and should have.

Louis E. Boone

Inaction breeds doubt and fear. Action breeds confidence and courage. If you want to conquer fear, do not sit home and think about it. Go out and get busy.

Dale Carnegie

You gain strength, courage, and confidence by every experience in which you really stop to look fear in the face. You must do the thing which you think you cannot do.

Eleanor Roosevelt

We can easily forgive a child who is afraid of the dark; the real tragedy of life is when men are afraid of the light.

Plato

If you're not willing to risk, you cannot grow. If you cannot grow, you cannot be your best. If you cannot be your best, you cannot be happy. If you cannot be happy, what else is there?

Les Brown

Never be afraid to try something new. Remember, amateurs built the ark, professionals built the Titanic.

Unknown

Fears are stories we tell ourselves.

Unknown

"Fear has two meanings: 'Forget Everything And Run' or 'Face Everything And Rise.' The choice is yours."

Zig Ziglar

Fear doesn't exist anywhere except in the mind.

Dale Carnegie

Living with fear stops us taking risks, and if you don't go out on the branch, you're never going to get the best fruit.

Sarah Parish

The greatest mistake we make is living in constant fear that we will make one.

John C. Maxwell

I must not fear. Fear is the mind-killer. Fear is the little-death that brings total obliteration. I will face my fear. I will permit it to pass over me and through me. And when it has gone past I will turn the inner eye to see its path. Where the fear has gone there will be nothing. Only I will remain.

Frank Herbert

Doubt kills more dreams than failure ever will.

Suzy Kassem

Ultimately we know deeply that that other side of every fear is a freedom.

Marilyn Ferguson

Only when we are no longer afraid do we begin to live.

Dorothy Thompson

He who has overcome his fears will truly be free.

Aristotle

A man who fears suffering is already suffering from what he fears.

Michel de Montaigne

I was never afraid of failure; for I would sooner fail than not be among the greatest.

John Keats

Fear is temporary. Regret is forever.

Unknown

The fears we don't face becomes our limits.

Robin Sharma

Do one thing every day that scares you.

Eleanor Roosevelt

Don't be afraid to give up the good to go for the great.

John D. Rockefeller

Courage is resistance to fear, mastery of fear, not absence of fear.

Mark Twain

I fear not the man who has practiced 10,000 kicks, but I fear the man who has practiced one kick 10,000 times.

Bruce Lee

The only thing we have to fear is fear itself.

Franklin D. Roosevelt

Courage is knowing what not to fear.

Plato

Limits, like fear, is often an illusion.

Michael Jordan

Thinking will not overcome fear but action will.

W. Clement Stone

Extreme fear can neither fight nor fly.

Williams Shakespeare

Beware; for I am fearless, and therefore powerful.

Mary Shelley (Frankenstein)

Let us never negotiate out of fear. But let us never fear to negotiate.

John F. Kennedy

Fear not the path of Truth for the lack of people walking on it.

Robert F. Kennedy

The purpose of life is to live it, to taste experience to the utmost, to reach out eagerly and without fear for newer and richer experience.

Eleanor Roosevelt

Keep your fears to yourself, but share your inspiration with others.

Robert Louis Stevenson

Don't fear failure. Fear the absence of progress.

Unknown

How very little can be done under the spirit of fear.

Florence Nightingale

Focus on where you want to go, not on what you fear.

Tony Robbins

Your largest fear carries your greatest growth.

Unknown

www.ingramcontent.com/pod-product-compliance
Lightning Source LLC
LaVergne TN
LVHW051248080426

835513LV00016B/1796